WINNERS'
Reading & Writing

2

Clue & Key

WINNERS' Reading & Writing ②

Scope & Sequence

Chapter		Unit	Topic		Reading
1	Animals	01	Pets	fiction	My Pets
		02	Zoo Animals	nonfiction	The Zoo
2	Weather & Seasons	03	Weather	fiction	This Week's Weather
		04	Seasons	nonfiction	Seasonal Activities
3	Free-Time Activities	05	After-School Activities	fiction	Busy! Busy! Busy!
		06	Fun Activities	nonfiction	Fun Things
4	Special Days	07	Outdoor Activities	fiction	A Day Out
		08	Various Holidays	nonfiction	Holidays
5	School	09	School Workers	fiction	School Workers
		10	Event Day	nonfiction	Sports Day
6	Places	11	Amusement Parks	fiction	The Amusement Park
		12	Public Places	nonfiction	Good Manners

Language Point	Writing	Writing Point
can / can't	Writing About My Pet	Apostrophe –The Contraction *can't*
adverbs	Writing a Report on My Favorite Zoo Animal	
It is + weather	Writing a Weather Report	Capitalization (1) – Days of the Week
in + season	Writing a Report on My Favorite Season	
3rd person + verb	Writing About My Friends' After-School Activities	Subject-Verb Agreement
like + -ing	Writing About an Activity That My Friend and I Like Doing	
let's...	Writing a Letter to My Friend	Capitalization (2) – Months & Holidays
in + month / on + day	Writing About My Family Members' Birthdays	
djective and adjective	Writing a Report on a School Worker	Abbreviation – *Mr.* & *Ms.*
on / in + place	Writing an Ad for a School Event	
present continuous	Describing Children's Activities at an Amusement Park	Gerunds
imperatives	Writing About the Rules in a Public Place	

How to Use
WINNERS' Reading & Writing ②

Student Book

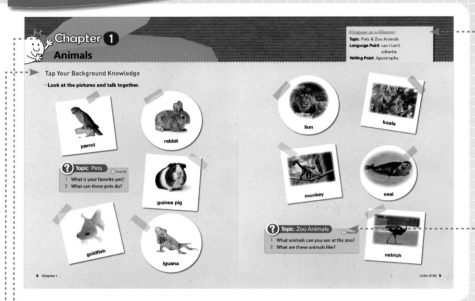

• Chapters

In the *WINNERS' Reading & Writing* Series, each book contains 6 big themes which are all divided into two topics. By reading and writing about a broad range of topics, students can obtain both thematic knowledge and language skills.

• Tap Your Background Knowledge

This section introduces basic vocabulary items related to the following two topics. By checking the basic words and corresponding pictures, students can learn new words and build their background knowledge of the topic at the same time. These words will also be a great help when students need additional vocabulary while doing the *Read & Write* section.

• Chapter at a Glance

Each chapter begins with a list of learning objectives so that teachers and students can preview the topics and language points presented in the chapter.

• Topic Questions

Questions about each topic help students preview each unit and build some background knowledge. By asking and answering questions together, both teachers and students can start the lesson in a relaxing and communicative way.

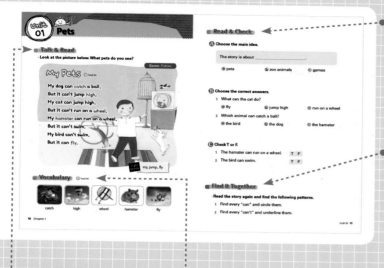

Read & Check

The set of comprehension questions that cover topics from finding the main idea to checking detailed information helps students fully understand the story.

Find It Together

After reading and understanding the story, students can use this section to find and recognize the main language point (the target grammar) in the story by themselves.

Talk & Read

Before reading, students can preview the story and predict what will happen while talking about the picture. Each chapter presents a fiction and a nonfiction story, which provide students with a good balance at an early stage of reading.

Vocabulary

Each unit introduces five new words from the main story in a format of picture dictionary.

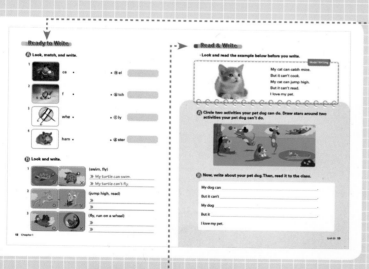

Ready to Write

Through level-appropriate activities, students can practice the target words and grammar of the unit in sentences.

Read & Write

The writing section begins with a model writing which shows the goal of the writing task. The topic and the model writing are given, but students can still choose their own interests or personalized contents for their writing. They can use the vocabulary and language point they learned, which enables teachers to check students' overall understanding of each unit. As students complete writing tasks in different genres or text types, they will be able to gain a lot of confidence and interest in writing. Feedback from peers will result in a more fun and productive writing lesson.

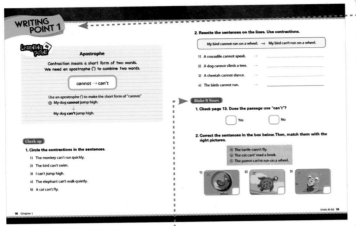

Writing Point

Each chapter ends with a special section for building writing accuracy with grammar and punctuation exercises. With clear and concise explanations and checkup exercises, students can be more confident while writing.

Make It Yours

This section enables students to apply what they have learned to their own writing. Students should be encouraged to refer back to the sentences they wrote and to check for mistakes by themselves. This proofreading and editing practice will lead students to become better writers and readers.

Workbook

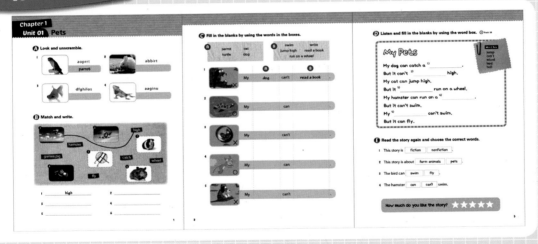

Workbook

The workbook is composed of three big sections: vocabulary practice, sentence structuring, and story review with dictation. By wrapping up the lesson through these exercises, students can reinforce their vocabulary, grammar, and listening skills.

You can download the MP3 files for this book from
www.clueandkey.com

CONTENTS

Chapter 1

Animals

Tap Your Background Knowledge

- **Look at the pictures and talk together.**

parrot

rabbit

? **Topic:** Pets

⊙ Track 02

1 What is your favorite pet?
2 What can these pets do?

guinea pig

goldfish

iguana

lion

koala

monkey

seal

ostrich

? **Topic**: Zoo Animals

⊙ Track 03

1 What animals can you see at the zoo?
2 What are these animals like?

Unit 01 Pets

Talk & Read

- **Look at the picture below. What pets do you see?**

Genre: Fiction

My Pets ◉ Track 04

My dog can catch a ball.

But it can't jump high.

My cat can jump high.

But it can't run on a wheel.

My hamster can run on a wheel.

But it can't swim.

My bird can't swim.

But it can fly.

Sight Words my, jump, fly

Vocabulary ◉ Track 05

| catch | high | wheel | hamster | fly |

Read & Check

A Choose the main idea.

The story is about _____.

  ⓐ pets   ⓑ zoo animals ⓒ games

B Choose the correct answers.

1 What can the cat do?

  ⓐ fly   ⓑ jump high ⓒ run on a wheel

2 Which animal can catch a ball?

  ⓐ the bird   ⓑ the dog ⓒ the hamster

C Check T or F.

1 The hamster can run on a wheel. T F

2 The bird can swim. T F

Find It Together

- **Read the story again and find the following patterns.**

1 Find every "can" and circle them.

2 Find every "can't" and underline them.

Ready to Write

A **Look, match, and write.**

1  ca •

• ⓐ el

2  f •

• ⓑ tch

3 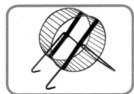 whe •

• ⓒ ly

4  ham •

• ⓓ ster

B **Look and write.**

1 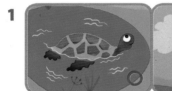 (swim, fly)

≫ My turtle can swim.

≫ My turtle can't fly.

2  (jump high, read)

≫ _____

≫ _____

3  (fly, run on a wheel)

≫ _____

≫ _____

Read & Write

- **Look and read the example below before you write.**

My cat can catch mice.

But it can't cook.

My cat can jump high.

But it can't read.

I love my pet.

A Circle two activities your pet dog can do. Draw stars around two activities your pet dog can't do.

B Now, write about your pet dog. Then, read it to the class.

My dog can _____.

But it can't _____.

My dog _____.

But it _____.

I love my pet.

Unit 02 Zoo Animals

Talk & Read

▪ **Look at the picture below. What zoo animals can you see?**

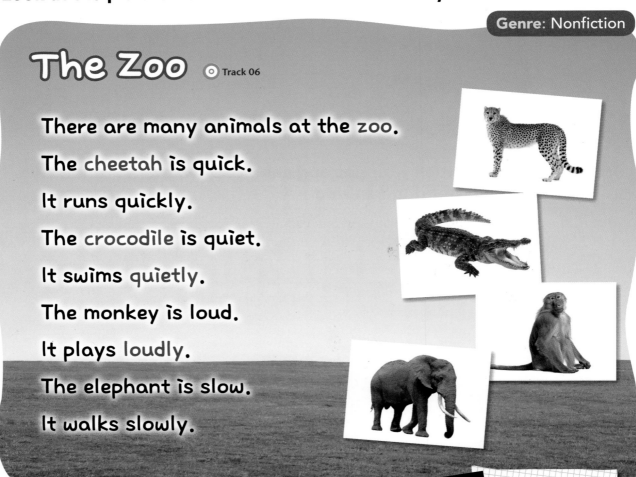

Genre: Nonfiction

The Zoo ⊙ Track 06

There are many animals at the zoo.

The cheetah is quick.

It runs quickly.

The crocodile is quiet.

It swims quietly.

The monkey is loud.

It plays loudly.

The elephant is slow.

It walks slowly.

Sight Words the, run, play

Vocabulary ⊙ Track 07

zoo   cheetah   crocodile   quietly   loudly

Read & Check

Ⓐ Choose the main idea.

The story is about _____.

ⓐ pets   ⓑ slow animals   ⓒ zoo animals

Ⓑ Choose the correct answers.

1   How does the cheetah run?

     ⓐ slowly   ⓑ quietly   ⓒ quickly

2   Which animal walks slowly?

     ⓐ the cheetah   ⓑ the elephant   ⓒ the crocodile

Ⓒ Check T or F.

1   The crocodile swims slowly.   **T**   **F**

2   The monkey plays loudly.   **T**   **F**

Find It Together

▪ **Read the story again and find the following patterns.**

1   Find the names of the animals and circle them.

2   Find the words with "-ly" and underline them.

Ready to Write

A Use the code to find out each word. Write it. Then, match.

1	2	3	4	5	6	7	8	9	10	11	12	13
a	b	c	d	e	f	g	h	i	j	k	l	m

14	15	16	17	18	19	20	21	22	23	24	25	26
n	o	p	q	r	s	t	u	v	w	x	y	z

1 3, 18, 15, 3, 15, 4, 9, 12, 5

•

_____

 •Ⓐ

2 3, 8, 5, 5, 20, 1, 8

•

_____

 •Ⓑ

3 12, 15, 21, 4, 12, 25

•

_____

 •Ⓒ

B Look and write.

1

(giraffe, walk, quietly)

» The giraffe walks quietly. _____

2

(koala, move, slowly)

» _____

3

(ostrich, run, quickly)

» _____

Read & Write

Look and read the report below before you write.

My favorite animal is the monkey.

The monkey plays loudly.

The monkey eats bananas quickly.

I love monkeys very much.

A **Look at the pictures and circle your favorite animal.**

eat apples quickly

play loudly

move smoothly

walk slowly

move slowly

swim quietly

B **Now, write a report on your favorite animal. Then, read it to the class.**

My favorite animal is _____.

The _____.

The _____.

I love _____.

WRITING POINT 1

Apostrophe

Contraction means a short form of two words.
We need an apostrophe (') to combine two words.

$$\boxed{\text{cannot} \rightarrow \text{can't}}$$

Use an apostrophe (') to make the short form of "cannot."

ex My dog **cannot** jump high.

↓

My dog **can't** jump high.

Check-up

1. Circle the contractions in the sentences.

1) The monkey can't run quickly.

2) The bird can't swim.

3) I can't jump high.

4) The elephant can't walk quietly.

5) A cat can't fly.

2. Rewrite the sentences on the lines. Use contractions.

> My bird cannot run on a wheel. ➡ My bird can't run on a wheel.

1) A crocodile cannot speak.   ···▶   _____

2) A dog cannot climb a tree.   ···▶   _____

3) A cheetah cannot dance.   ···▶   _____

4) The birds cannot run.   ···▶   _____

Make It Yours

1. Check page 13. Does the passage use "can't"?

◯ Yes   ◯ No

2. Correct the sentences in the box below. Then, match them with the right pictures.

> ⓐ The turtle cann't fly.
> ⓑ The cat cant' read a book.
> ⓒ The parrot can'nt run on a wheel.

1)

2)

3)

Chapter **2**
Weather & Seasons

Tap Your Background Knowledge

- **Look at the pictures and talk together.**

foggy

cloudy

? **Topic**: Weather

◎ Track 08

1 What kind of weather do you like?
2 How is the weather today?

windy

snowy

rainy

**spring /
look at flowers**

**summer /
go to the beach**

**fall /
read books**

**winter /
play in the snow**

? **Topic**: Seasons

 Track 09

1 What is your favorite season?
2 What do you do during that season?

Talk & Read

■ **Look at the picture below. How is the weather?**

Genre: Fiction

Monday	Tuesday	Wednesday	Thursday	Friday

This Week's Weather ◎ Track 10

Sarah reads the weather report.

On Monday, it is hot and sunny.

On Tuesday, it is warm and cloudy.

On Wednesday, it is rainy and windy.

On Thursday, it is cool and stormy.

On Friday, it is hot and sunny again.

Sight Words on, hot, warm

Vocabulary ◎ Track 11

weather report

sunny

warm

cool

stormy

Read & Check

A **Choose the main idea.**

The story is about _____.

    ⓐ rain   ⓑ the weather   ⓒ Sarah

B **Choose the correct answers.**

1 How is the weather on Monday?

    ⓐ sunny and rainy   ⓑ warm and cloudy   ⓒ hot and sunny

2 Which day is rainy?

    ⓐ Tuesday   ⓑ Wednesday   ⓒ Friday

C **Check T or F.**

1 It is stormy on Friday.   T   F

2 The weather is cloudy on Tuesday.   T   F

Find It Together

▪ **Read the story again and find the following patterns.**

1 Find the weather words and circle them.

2 Find every "it is" and underline them.

Ready to Write

A **Use the code to find out each word. Write it. Then, match.**

1	2	3	4	5	6	7	8	9	10	11	12	13
a	b	c	d	e	f	g	h	i	j	k	l	m

14	15	16	17	18	19	20	21	22	23	24	25	26
n	o	p	q	r	s	t	u	v	w	x	y	z

1 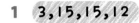 3, 15, 15, 12

_____•   •ⓐ

2 19, 20, 15, 18, 13, 25

_____•   •ⓑ

3 19, 21, 14, 14, 25

_____•   •ⓒ

B **Look and write.**

1  (cold, snowy)

》 It is cold and snowy. _____

2 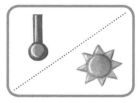 (hot, sunny)

》 _____

3  (cool, windy)

》 _____

Read & Write

- **Look and read the weather report below before you write.**

The Weather Report for Sunday

Here is Sunday's weather.

This morning, it is cool and sunny.

This afternoon, it is cold and windy.

This evening, it is cold and snowy.

A Look at the weather report for Saturday and Sunday. Then, choose the day you want to write about.

	Morning		Afternoon		Evening	
Saturday	warm	sunny	hot	sunny	cool	rainy
Sunday	cool	foggy	windy	rainy	cold	stormy

B Now, write a weather report. Then, read it to the class.

The Weather Report for _____

Here is _____ .

This morning, it is _____ .

This afternoon, _____ .

This evening, _____ .

Unit 04 Seasons

Talk & Read

- **Look at the picture below. What activities do you see?**

Genre: Nonfiction

Seasonal Activities ⊙ Track 12

What do people do in each season?

The girls pick strawberries in spring.

The boys play in the rain in summer.

The girls make pumpkin pies in fall.

The boys ski in winter.

They enjoy all of the seasons.

Sight Words in, pick, make

Vocabulary ⊙ Track 13

pick

spring

pumpkin pie

ski

winter

Read & Check

A Choose the main idea.

The story is about _____.

ⓐ favorite seasons   ⓑ skiing   ⓒ activities in seasons

B Choose the correct answers.

1　What do the girls do in spring?

ⓐ pick strawberries　　ⓑ ski　　　　ⓒ make pumpkin pies

2　When do the boys play in the rain?

ⓐ spring　　　　　ⓑ summer　　　ⓒ fall

C Check T or F.

1　The girls make pumpkin pies in fall.　　T　F

2　The boys ski in spring.　　T　F

Find It Together

▪ **Read the story again and find the following patterns.**

1　Find every "in" and circle them.

2　Find the seasons and underline them.

Ready to Write

A Look, match, and write.

1

spr •

• ⓐ ter

2

pi •

• ⓑ ing

3

win •

• ⓒ ck

4

sk •

• ⓓ i

B Look and write.

1

(we, sled, winter)

》 We sled in winter.

2

(they, look at flowers, spring)

》 _____

3

(I, read books, fall)

》 _____

Read & Write

- **Look and read the report below before you write.**

My favorite season is summer.

I go to the beach in summer.

I also play in the rain in summer.

Summer is the best season.

A **Draw two things you do in your favorite season.**

B **Now, write a report on your favorite season. Then, present it to the class.**

My favorite season is _____.
(season)

I _____ in _____.
(activity)   (season)

I also _____.

_____ is the best season.

WRITING POINT 2

Capitalization (1)

We have to start some words with capital letters.
The names of the days begin with capital letters.

> **M**onday   **T**uesday   **W**ednesday
>
> **T**hursday   **F**riday   **S**aturday   **S**unday

Always write the first letter of a day of the week with a capital letter.

ex   My favorite day of the week is **S**aturday.

I like **M**ondays.

Check-up

1. Circle the days of the week. Then, write the words on the lines. Use capital letters.

1) money   monday   mommy   _____

2) rainy   snowy   wednesday   _____

3) sunday   someday   everyday   _____

4) afternoon   thursday   evening   _____

5) friday   summer   spring   _____

2. Rewrite the sentences on the lines. Use capital letters for the days of the week.

> On monday, the weather is sunny. ➡ On Monday, the weather is sunny.

1) It is cloudy on saturday. ⋯➤ _____

2) We can ski on thursday. ⋯➤ _____

3) The party is on wednesday. ⋯➤ _____

4) Do you like tuesday or sunday? ⋯➤ _____

Make It Yours

1. Check page 25. Do the days of the week start with capital letters?

☐ Yes   ☐ No

2. Correct the sentences in the box below. Then, match them with the right pictures.

> ⓐ It's snowy on tuesday.
> ⓑ On friday, it's rainy.
> ⓒ On saturday, it's sunny.

1)

2)

3)

Free-Time Activities

Tap Your Background Knowledge

▪ **Look at the pictures and talk together.**

meet friends

play hide and seek

> **?** **Topic**: After-School Activities
>
> ◉ Track 14
> 1 What do you do after school?
> 2 What after-school activities do you enjoy?

do homework

practice the piano

bake cookies

Chapter at a Glance

Topic: After-School Activities & Fun Activities
Language Point: [3rd person+verb]
[like+-ing]
Writing Point: Subject-Verb Agreement

play board games

blow bubbles

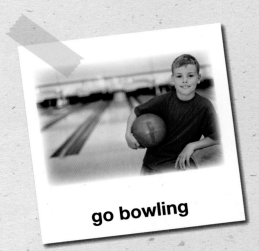

go bowling

ride bikes

? Topic: Fun Activities

Track 15

1 Which activities are fun?
2 What do you like doing?

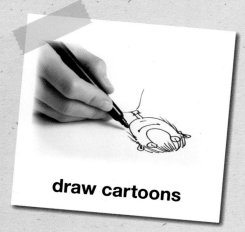

draw cartoons

Unit 05 After-School Activities

Talk & Read

▪ Look at the picture below. What activities are they doing?

Genre: Fiction

Busy! Busy! Busy! ⊙ Track 16

We are busy after school.

I play soccer after school.

Olivia meets her friends after school.

John practices the piano after school.

He also does his homework.

Becky bakes cookies after school.

We are so tired.

Sight Words after, school, does

Vocabulary ⊙ Track 17

 soccer

 meet

 homework

 bake

 tired

Read & Check

A Choose the main idea.

The story is about _____.

ⓐ school   ⓑ after-school activities   ⓒ homework

B Choose the correct answers.

1 What does Olivia do after school?

ⓐ meets her friends   ⓑ does her homework   ⓒ plays soccer

2 Who practices the piano after school?

ⓐ John   ⓑ I   ⓒ Becky

C Check T or F.

1 Becky bakes cookies after school.   T   F

2 They are not busy after school.   T   F

Find It Together

▪ **Read the story again and find the following patterns.**

1 Find every "after school" and circle them.

2 Find the after-school activities and underline them.

Ready to Write

A Look, match, and write.

1  ba •   • ⓐ et

2  me •   • ⓑ red

3  ti •   • ⓒ cer

4  soc •   • ⓓ ke

B Look and write.

1

(use her computer)

» *She uses her computer.*
_____

2

(practice the piano)

»
_____

3

(bake cookies)

»
_____

Read & Write

Look and read the example below before you write.

My friends do many activities after school.

Paul uses his computer after school.

Jamie bakes cookies after school.

Peter plays soccer after school.

A **Talk to your friends and fill in the blanks.**

Find someone who...

name

• bakes cookies after school   _____

• meets his/her friends after school   _____

• practices the piano after school   _____

• does his/her homework after school   _____

B **Now, write about your friends' after-school activities. Then, read it to the class.**

My friends do many activities after school.

_____ _____ after school.

   (name)   (activity)

_____ after school.

_____ after school.

Talk & Read

▪ Look at the picture below. What activities do you see?

Genre: Nonfiction

Fun Things 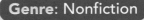 Track 18

There are many fun things everywhere.

The students all like blowing bubbles.

They also like drawing cartoons.

The boys like riding their bikes in the park.

The girls like playing board games.

All of the activities are so much fun.

 Sight Words there, like, much

Vocabulary  Track 19

fun	blow	bubble	cartoon	board game

A **Choose the main idea.**

The story is about _____.

ⓐ fun activities   ⓑ playing games   ⓒ seasonal activities

B **Choose the correct answers.**

1   What do the students all like doing?

ⓐ playing board games

ⓑ blowing bubbles

ⓒ riding their bikes

2   Where do the boys like riding their bikes?

ⓐ in the park   ⓑ in the yard   ⓒ in the house

C **Check T or F.**

1   The students like drawing cartoons.   T   F

2   All of the activities are fun.   T   F

Find It Together

▪ **Read the story again and find the following patterns.**

1   Find every "like" and circle them.

2   Find the activities and underline them.

Ready to Write

A **Use the code to find out each word. Write it. Then, match.**

1	2	3	4	5	6	7	8	9	10	11	12	13
a	b	c	d	e	f	g	h	i	j	k	l	m

14	15	16	17	18	19	20	21	22	23	24	25	26
n	o	p	q	r	s	t	u	v	w	x	y	z

1 2, 21, 2, 2, 12, 5

_____   •   • ⓐ

2 2, 12, 15, 23

_____   •   • ⓑ

3 3, 1, 18, 20, 15, 15, 14

_____   •   • ⓒ

B **Look and write.**

1  (Kate, cook)

» Kate likes cooking. _____

2  (we, play board games)

» _____

3  (they, blow bubbles)

» _____

Read & Write

▪ **Look and read the example below before you write.**

Laura likes playing basketball.

I like playing basketball, too.

We like playing basketball together.

A **Check the activities that you like doing. Then, ask your friend what he/she likes doing.**

	draw cartoons	play board games	go bowling	blow bubbles
You				
Your Friend				

B **Now, write about what you and your friend both like doing. Then, read it to the class.**

_____ likes _____ .
(friend's name)   (activity)

I like _____ .

We _____ .

WRITING POINT 3

Subject-Verb Agreement

Sometimes we have to change the endings of verbs.

| I **play** soccer. | She **plays** soccer. |

- When the subject is *I*, *you*, *we*, or *they*, just write the regular form of the verb.
  - ex I **play** the piano after school.
    They **bake** cookies every day.

- When the subject is *he*, *she*, or *it*, add *-s* or *-es* to the end of the verb.
  - ex He **plays** the piano after school.
    She **bakes** cookies every day.

meet → meets	write → writes
practice → practices	do → does
draw → draws	go → goes

Check-up

1. Choose the correct words.

1) Joe (practice / practices) the piano every day.

2) I (meets / meet) my friends on Monday.

3) She (draw / draws) cartoons.

4) Sarah (like / likes) playing board games.

5) He (do / does) his math homework after school.

2. Rewrite the sentences on the lines. Change the verbs correctly.

> Paul use his computer. ➡ Paul uses his computer.

1) Mark like reading books. ····▶ _____

2) Mary go to school every day. ····▶ _____

3) We eats lunch at twelve. ····▶ _____

4) He write a letter to his parents. ····▶ _____

Make It Yours

1. Check page 37. Do the verbs that come after *he*, *she*, and *it* end with *-s* or *-es*?

◯ Yes ◯ No

2. Correct the sentences in the box below. Then, match them with the right pictures.

> ⓐ Sue meet her friend after school.
> ⓑ Chris play board games.
> ⓒ Jamie blow bubbles.

1)

2)

3)

Chapter 4

Special Days

Tap Your Background Knowledge

- **Look at the pictures and talk together.**

go to a water park

fly a kite

? Topic: Outdoor Activities

⊙ Track 20

1 What do you like to do outside?
2 What is your favorite outdoor activity?

go camping

throw the Frisbee

have a picnic

Chapter at a Glance

Topic: Outdoor Activities & Various Holidays
Language Point: [let's...]
[in+month / on+day]
Writing Point: Capitalization (2)

New Year's Day

Thanksgiving

Mother's Day

Father's Day

? Topic: Various Holidays

◉ Track 21

1 What is your favorite holiday?
2 When is that holiday?

Christmas

Unit 07

Outdoor Activities

Talk & Read

▪ **Look at the picture below. What do the children do?**

Genre: Fiction

A Day Out ⊙ Track 22

Tim and Mary are at the park.

They like playing outside.

"Let's have a picnic," says Mary.

"Sorry. I'm not hungry," answers Tim.

"Let's throw the Frisbee," says Tim.

"No, it's very hot, let's swim," answers Mary.

"Great idea. Let's go!"

Sight Words at, let, idea

Vocabulary ⊙ Track 23

| outside | throw | Frisbee | swim | idea |

Read & Check

A **Choose the main idea.**

The story is about _____.

   ⓐ having a picnic   ⓑ playing outside   ⓒ Mary's friend

B **Choose the correct answers.**

1 Where are Tim and Mary?

   ⓐ in the yard   ⓑ at the park   ⓒ at school

2 How is the weather?

   ⓐ hot   ⓑ cold   ⓒ snowy

C **Check T or F.**

1 Tim is hungry.   **T F**

2 Mary says, "Let's have a picnic."   **T F**

Find It Together

▪ **Read the story again and find the following patterns.**

1 Find every "Let's" and circle them.

2 Find "let's swim" and underline it.

Ready to Write

A Use the code to find out each word. Write it. Then, match.

1	2	3	4	5	6	7	8	9	10	11	12	13
a	b	c	d	e	f	g	h	i	j	k	l	m

14	15	16	17	18	19	20	21	22	23	24	25	26
n	o	p	q	r	s	t	u	v	w	x	y	z

1 15, 21, 20, 19, 9, 4, 5

_____   •

• ⓐ

2 20, 8, 18, 15, 23

_____   •

• ⓑ

3 19, 23, 9, 13

_____   •

• ⓒ

B Look and write.

1

(fish in the lake)

≫ Let's fish in the lake.
_____

2

(fly a kite)

≫ _____

3

(go to a water park)

≫ _____

Read & Write

Look and read the letter below before you write.

Dear Jim,

Let's have a picnic tomorrow.
And let's fly a kite.
See you soon.

Steve

A **Choose two activities you want to do with your friend outside.**

go camping   fly a kite   go to a water park   have a picnic

B **Now, write a letter to your friend about the activities you want to do. Then, read it to the class.**

Dear _____,
     (your friend's name)

Let's _____.

And _____.

See you soon.

_____
   (your name)

Unit 08 Various Holidays

Talk & Read

- **Look at the picture below. What holidays do you see?**

Holidays ⊙ Track 24

There are many holidays around the world.

Let's look at the calendar.

New Year's Day is in January.

It is on Tuesday.

Father's Day is in June.

It is on Sunday.

Christmas is in December.

It is on Monday.

Sight Words   many, around, on

Vocabulary ⊙ Track 25

| world | calendar | January | Sunday | December |

Read & Check

A Choose the main idea.

The story is about _____.

    ⓐ Christmas   ⓑ months   ⓒ holidays

B Choose the correct answers.

1 When is New Year's Day?

    ⓐ January   ⓑ December   ⓒ February

2 Which holiday is in June?

    ⓐ New Year's Day   ⓑ Father's Day   ⓒ Christmas

C Check T or F.

1 Christmas is in April.   T   F

2 New Year's Day and Father's Day are in the same month.   T   F

Find It Together

▪ **Read the story again and find the following patterns.**

1 Find the months and underline them.

2 Find every "in" and circle them.

3 Find every "on" and draw stars on them.

Ready to Write

A Look, match, and write.

1  Sun •   • ⓐ dar

2  wo •   • ⓑ ber

3 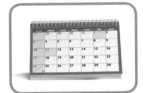 calen •   • ⓒ rld

4  Decem •   • ⓓ day

B Look and write.

1  (New Year's Eve)

» New Year's Eve is in December.

» It is on Monday.

2 (Thanksgiving)

»

»

3 (Mother's Day)

»

»

Read & Write

■ **Look and read the example below before you write.**

Birthdays are special days.

My mother's birthday is in August.

It's on Friday.

My brother's birthday is in April.

It's on Sunday.

A **Write the dates of your family members' birthdays. Then, look at the calendar and fill in the blanks.**

Family Member	Birthday	Day of the Week
my sister	November 1	Sunday

B **Now, write about your family members' birthdays. Then, read it to the class.**

Birthdays are special days.

My _____'s birthday is _____.
           (family member)   (month)

It's _____.
                 (day)

My _____'s birthday is _____.

It's _____.

Capitalization (2)

We need to start some words with capital letters.

> **F**ebruary   **F**ather's **D**ay

- Months – Always write the first letter of a month with a capital letter.

  ex My birthday is in **M**ay.
  School starts in **S**eptember.

January	February	March	April
May	June	July	August
September	October	November	December

- Holidays – Always write the first letter of a holiday with a capital letter.

  ex Her favorite holiday is **C**hristmas.
  New **Y**ear's **D**ay is in January.

Check-up

1. Write the correct letters in the blanks.

1)
　☐hristmas

2) **4**
S	M	T	W	T	F	S
						1
2	3	4	5	6	7	8
9	10	11	12	13	14	15
16	17	18	19	20	21	22
23	24	25	26	27	28	29
30						
　☐pril

3) **12**
S	M	T	W	T	F	S
						1
2	3	4	5	6	7	8
9	10	11	12	13	14	15
16	17	18	19	20	21	22
23	24	25	26	27	28	29
30	31					
　☐ecember

4)
　☐other's ☐ay

5)
　☐hanksgiving

6) **8**
S	M	T	W	T	F	S
		1	2	3	4	5
6	7	8	9	10	11	12
13	14	15	16	17	18	19
20	21	22	23	24	25	26
27	28	29	30	31		
　☐ugust

2. Rewrite the sentences on the lines. Use capital letters when they are needed.

1) We bake cookies on mother's day. ····▶ _____

2) They go camping in april. ····▶ _____

3) I go to a water park in august. ····▶ _____

4) Father's day is on Sunday. ····▶ _____

5) Lisa's favorite month is october. ····▶ _____

Make It Yours

1. Check page 53. Do the months and days start with capital letters?

⬜ Yes   ⬜ No

2. Correct the sentences in the box below. Then, match them with the right pictures.

> ⓐ Kate's birthday is in september.
> ⓑ My favorite holiday is thanksgiving.
> ⓒ We swim in june and july.

1)

2)

3)

Chapter 5
School

Tap Your Background Knowledge

- **Look at the pictures and talk together.**

teacher / kind

coach / funny

? Topic: School Workers　　⊙ Track 26

1　Who works at your school?
2　What does each school worker do?

school nurse / smart

lunch lady / friendly

driver / helpful

Chapter at a Glance

Topic: School Workers & Event Day
Language Point: [adjective and adjective]
[on / in + place]
Writing Point: Abbreviation

field trip

bake sale

sports day

talent show

? **Topic**: Event Day

Track 27

1 What events does your school have?
2 What is your favorite school event?

graduation

School Workers

Talk & Read

■ Look at the picture below. Who are they?

Genre: Fiction

School Workers ⊙ Track 28

Furi loves the school workers.

Mr. Zoozica is Furi's teacher.

He is kind and smart.

Ms. Poppet is the principal.

She is funny and nice.

Mr. Mookle is the librarian.

He is friendly and helpful.

They are all great.

Sight Words is, kind, all

Vocabulary ⊙ Track 29

| smart | principal | librarian | helpful | great |

Read & Check

A **Choose the main idea.**

The story is about _____.

ⓐ schools   ⓑ school workers   ⓒ students

B **Choose the correct answers.**

1   How is Ms. Poppet?

   ⓐ friendly   ⓑ smart   ⓒ funny

2   Who is helpful?

   ⓐ Mr. Mookle   ⓑ Mr. Zoozica   ⓒ Furi

C **Check T or F.**

1   Mr. Zoozica is kind and funny.   T   F

2   The principal is nice.   T   F

Find It Together

▪ **Read the story again and find the following patterns.**

1   Find all the names of school workers and circle them.

2   Find all the words that tell you about the school workers. Then, underline them.

Ready to Write

A Use the code to find out each word. Write it. Then, match.

1	2	3	4	5	6	7	8	9	10	11	12	13
a	b	c	d	e	f	g	h	i	j	k	l	m

14	15	16	17	18	19	20	21	22	23	24	25	26
n	o	p	q	r	s	t	u	v	w	x	y	z

1 8, 5, 12, 16, 6, 21, 12

_____ •

•ⓐ

2 19, 13, 1, 18, 20

_____ •

•ⓑ

3 16, 18, 9, 14, 3, 9, 16, 1, 12

_____ •

•ⓒ

B Look and write.

1  (builder, friendly, helpful)

》 The builder is friendly and helpful.
_____

2  (teacher, kind, smart)

》
_____

3  (principal, helpful, funny)

》
_____

Read & Write

- **Look and read the report below before you write.**

Ms. Simmons is a math teacher.
She is quiet and friendly.
She is also very funny.

A Draw a school worker. Then, circle three words you want to use.

kind

funny

smart

quiet

friendly

helpful

nice

B Write a report on the school worker. Then, present it to the class.

_____ _____ is _____ _____.
(Mr. / Ms.)   (name)   (a / an)   (job)

_____ is _____ and _____.
(She / He)

_____ is also very _____.

Event Day

Talk & Read

- Look at the picture below. What event can you see?

Genre: Nonfiction

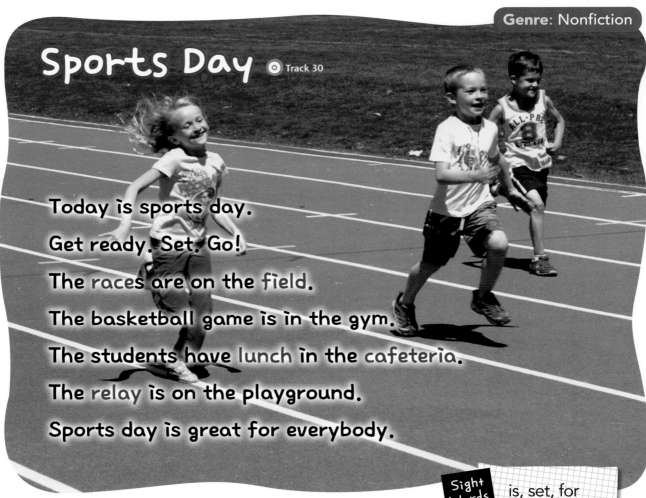

Sports Day ◉ Track 30

Today is sports day.

Get ready. Set. Go!

The races are on the field.

The basketball game is in the gym.

The students have lunch in the cafeteria.

The relay is on the playground.

Sports day is great for everybody.

Sight Words is, set, for

Vocabulary ◉ Track 31

| race | field | lunch | cafeteria | relay |

Read & Check

A **Choose the main idea.**

The story is about _____.

ⓐ lunchtime ⓑ sports day ⓒ races

B **Choose the correct answers.**

1 What is on the field?

ⓐ the relay ⓑ the races ⓒ lunch

2 Where is the basketball game?

ⓐ in the gym ⓑ on the field ⓒ on the playground

C **Check T or F.**

1 The students have lunch in the gym. T F

2 The relay is on the playground. T F

Find It Together

▪ **Read the story again and find the following patterns.**

1 Find the places and circle them.

2 Find every "on" and "in." Then, underline them.

Ready to Write

A Look, match, and write.

1  ra •   • ⓐ ch

2  lun •   • ⓑ eld

3  fi •   • ⓒ ria

4  cafete •   • ⓓ ce

B Look and write.

1  (school play, gym)

>> The school play is in the gym.

2  (graduation, field)

>>

3  (lunch, cafeteria)

>>

Read & Write

- **Look and read the ad below before you write.**

Come to the School Bake Sale.

What Month: It is in May.
What Day: It is on Friday.
Where: It is in the cafeteria.
Come and have fun!

A **Choose the school event you want to have.**

talent show / playground

graduation / gym

sports day / field

B **Now, write an ad for your school event. Then, read it to the class.**

Come to _____.

What Month: _____

What Day: _____

Where: _____

Come and have fun!

Abbreviation

An abbreviation is making a word in a short form.
An abbreviation starts with a capital letter and ends with a period.

Mr.   **Ms.**

- Mr. : This is a title for a man. Always capitalize the "M." And use a period (.) at the end.

  ex His teacher is **Mr.** Davis.

- Ms. : This is a title for a woman. Always capitalize the "M." And use a period (.) at the end.

  ex We all like **Ms.** Simmons.

Check-up

1. Circle the titles in the sentences. Then, write them on the lines.

1) The school librarian is Ms. Jenkins.

2) Is Mr. Smith the math teacher?

3) What does Mr. Wilson do?

4) Let's talk to Ms. Peters.

5) Mr. Kim is always busy.

2. Rewrite the sentences on the lines. Use capital letters and periods.

> ms Stewart teaches English. ➡ Ms. Stewart teaches English.

1) Where does mr Arnold work? ⋯▸ _____

2) Is ms Carter helpful? ⋯▸ _____

3) mr Richards is kind and funny. ⋯▸ _____

4) I want to meet ms Maple. ⋯▸ _____

Make It Yours

1. Check page 61. Does the passage use "Mr." or "Ms."?

◯ Yes   ◯ No

2. Correct the sentences in the box below. Then, match them with the right pictures.

> ⓐ The driver is mr Perkins.
> ⓑ mr. Taylor is the teacher.
> ⓒ Ms Reynolds is the librarian.

1)

2)

3)

Chapter 6

Places

Tap Your Background Knowledge

- **Look at the pictures and talk together.**

drive bumper cars

buy tickets

? Topic: Amusement Parks

Track 32

1 How do you like the amusement park?

2 What is your favorite ride?

ride on a
roller coaster

eat cotton candy

take pictures

shopping center

theater

park

subway

? **Topic**: Public Places

Track 33

1 Which public places do you visit?

2 How do you act in public places?

library

Talk & Read

■ Look at the picture below. Where are the children? What are they doing?

Genre: Fiction

The Amusement Park ⊙ Track 34

Look! We are at the amusement park.

I am not buying tickets.

I am driving a bumper car.

Mark is riding on the roller coaster.

He is smiling.

Amy is eating cotton candy.

Oh! It is very sweet!

Sight Words | look, am, not

Vocabulary ⊙ Track 35

amusement park

ticket

bumper car

roller coaster

cotton candy

Read & Check

A **Choose the main idea.**

The story is about _____.

    ⓐ games   ⓑ school activities   ⓒ an amusement park

B **Choose the correct answers.**

1   What is Mark riding on?

    ⓐ the bumper car   ⓑ the roller coaster   ⓒ the Ferris wheel

2   What is Amy doing?

    ⓐ buying tickets

    ⓑ eating cotton candy

    ⓒ driving a bumper car

C **Check T or F.**

1   Mark is smiling.   T   F

2   The cotton candy tastes very salty.   T   F

Find It Together

▪ **Read the story again and find the following patterns.**

1   Find the amusement park rides and circle them.

2   Find all the activity words ending with "-ing" and underline them.

Ready to Write

A Look, match, and write.

1  tic •   • ⓐ coaster

2  cotton •   • ⓑ candy

3  bumper •   • ⓒ ket

4  roller •   • ⓓ car

B Look and write.

1  (Jamie, ride on the Ferris wheel)

» *Jamie is riding on the Ferris wheel.*

_____

2  (Josh, take pictures)

»

_____

3  (Pitt, eat cotton candy)

»

_____

Read & Write

Look and read the example below before you write.

The children are at *Dream Land*.

Emily is riding on the Ferris wheel.

Simon is taking pictures.

Peter is eating cotton candy.

They are smiling.

A **Look at the picture and talk about what the children are doing.**

Chris and Becky

Jane

Jim

B **Now, describe the picture. Then, read it to the class.**

The children are at *Dream Land*.

_____

_____

_____

_____

Unit 12 Public Places

Talk & Read

- Look at the picture below. What does each sign say?

Genre: Nonfiction

Good Manners ● Track 36

There are rules on the sign.

⟨At a Bus Stop⟩

1. Wait for your turn.
2. Don't push others.
3. Don't yell.

⟨At a Library⟩

1. Walk quietly.
2. Don't talk loudly.
3. Don't eat any snacks.

Let's have good manners in public places.

Sight Words your, walk, eat

Vocabulary ● Track 37

sign

bus stop

push

yell

snack

A Choose the main idea.

The story is about _____.

ⓐ snacks

ⓑ walking quietly

ⓒ rules in public places

B Choose the correct answers.

1 Which is a public place?

ⓐ a home   ⓑ a car   ⓒ a library

2 What is a rule at a library?

ⓐ Yell.   ⓑ Talk loudly.   ⓒ Walk quietly.

C Check T or F.

1 Bus stops are public places.   T F

2 We can yell at a bus stop.   T F

Find It Together

▪ **Read the story again and find the following patterns.**

1 Find all the public places and circle them.

2 Find every "Don't" and underline them.

Ready to Write

A **Use the code to find out each word. Write it. Then, match.**

1	2	3	4	5	6	7	8	9	10	11	12	13
a	b	c	d	e	f	g	h	i	j	k	l	m

14	15	16	17	18	19	20	21	22	23	24	25	26
n	o	p	q	r	s	t	u	v	w	x	y	z

1 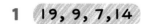 19, 9, 7, 14

_____

•   • ⓐ

2 25, 5, 12, 12

_____

•   • ⓑ

3 16, 21, 19, 8

_____

•   • ⓒ

B **Look and write.**

1    (fight)

   » Don't fight. _____

2    (yell)

   » _____

3    (eat any snacks)

   » _____

Read & Write

Look and read the sign before you write.

Model Writing

Fun Fun Theater Rules

1. Don't take pictures.
2. Don't run.
3. Don't eat or drink.

A Draw a public place you visit every day. Then, circle the sign posts you want to write about.

eat or drink   pick flowers   talk loudly

take pictures   run

B Now, write the rules for the public place. Then, present it to the class.

_____ **Rules**

1. _____

2. _____

3. _____

WRITING POINT 6

Gerunds

Sometimes we add -ing to verbs. We call these verbs gerunds.

jump → jump**ing**

make → mak**ing**

- When the verbs do not end with **-e**, add **-ing** to the end.

  ex We are eat**ing** bananas now. (eat → eating)

- When the verbs end with **-e**, delete the **-e**. Then, add **-ing** to the end.

  ex Karen is smil**ing** now. (smile → smiling)

buy → buying   take → taking
draw → drawing   ride → riding
go → going   drive → driving

Check-up

1. Change the verbs into gerunds.

1) take ····▸ _____

2) go ····▸ _____

3) sing ····▸ _____

4) ride ····▸ _____

5) drive ····▸ _____

6) eat ····▸ _____

7) jump ····▸ _____

8) make ····▸ _____

9) smile ····▸ _____

10) draw ····▸ _____

2. Correct the underlined words. Then, rewrite the sentences on the lines.

> My grandfather is <u>smileing</u>. ➡ My grandfather is smiling.

1) They are <u>talkiing</u> loudly. ┄➤ _____

2) Sara is not <u>buyeing</u> tickets. ┄➤ _____

3) We are <u>rideing</u> on the Ferris wheel. ┄➤ _____

4) Carolyn is <u>eatting</u> cotton candy. ┄➤ _____

Make It Yours

1. Check page 73. Do the verbs have -*ing* at the end?

☐ Yes   ☐ No

2. Correct the sentences in the box below. Then, match them with the right pictures.

ⓐ Amanda is eatiing cotton candy.
ⓑ Tom is driveing the bumper car.
ⓒ Gordon is takeing pictures.

1)

2)

3)

MEMO

Enjoy reading, then start writing with confidence!

WINNERS'
Reading & Writing
Workbook

2

Clue & Key

A Look and unscramble.

1   aoprrt
    parrot

2   abbirt

3   dfghilos

4   aaginu

B Match and write.

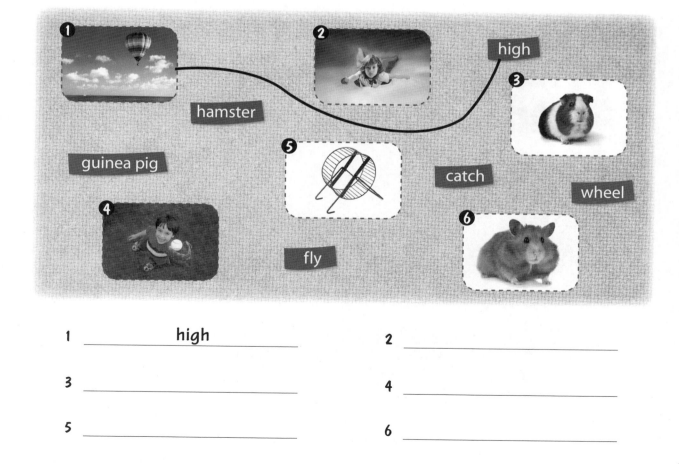

high

hamster

guinea pig

catch

wheel

fly

1 _____ high _____   2 _____

3 _____   4 _____

5 _____   6 _____

C Fill in the blanks by using the words in the boxes.

A

parrot   cat

turtle   dog

B

swim   write

jump high   read a book

run on a wheel

1. My   **A** *dog*   can't   **B** *read a book*   .

2. My   can   .

3. My   can't   .

4. My   can   .

5. My   can't   .

D Listen and fill in the blanks by using the word box. ◎ Track 38

My Pets

My dog can catch a ¹⁾ _____ .

But it can't ²⁾ _____ high.

My cat can jump high.

But it ³⁾ _____ run on a wheel.

My hamster can run on a ⁴⁾ _____ .

But it can't swim.

My ⁵⁾ _____ can't swim.

But it can fly.

Word Box

jump
can't
wheel
bird
ball

E Read the story again and choose the correct words.

1 This story is | fiction | nonfiction |.

2 This story is about | farm animals | pets |.

3 The bird can | swim | fly |.

4 The hamster | can | can't | swim.

How much do you like the story?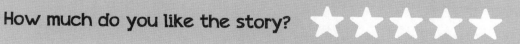

A Look, choose, and write.

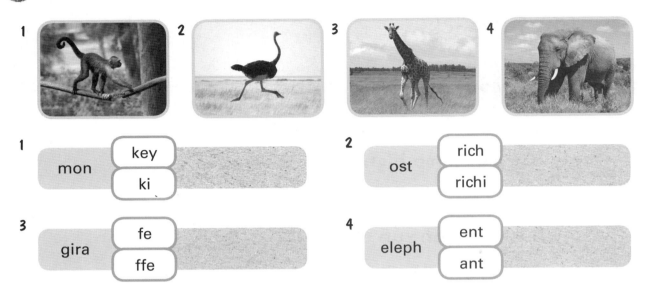

1 mon key / ki _____

2 ost rich / richi _____

3 gira fe / ffe _____

4 eleph ent / ant _____

B Match and write.

quietly zoo koala loudly cheetah crocodile

1 _____ 2 _____

3 _____ 4 _____

5 _____ 6 _____

C Fill in the blanks by using the words in the box.

slow　　smoothly　　quickly　　slowly　　loud　　quiet

1

The koala is slow.
It moves _____ slowly _____.

2

The monkey is _____.
It plays loudly.

3

The cheetah is quick.
It runs _____.

4

The giraffe is _____.
It walks quietly.

5

The seal is smooth.
It swims _____.

6

The elephant is _____.
It walks slowly.

D **Listen and fill in the blanks by using the word box.** 🔘 Track 39

The Zoo

There are many animals at the zoo.

The ¹⁾ _____ is quick.

It ²⁾ _____ quickly.

The crocodile is ³⁾ _____.

It swims quietly.

The monkey is loud.

It ⁴⁾ _____ loudly.

The elephant is slow.

It walks ⁵⁾ _____.

Word Box

slowly
plays
runs
quiet
cheetah

E **Read the story again and choose the correct words.**

1 This story is | fiction | nonfiction | .

2 This story is about | zoo animals | pets | .

3 The monkey plays | loud | loudly | .

4 The crocodile swims | quietly | slowly | .

How much do you like the story?

6

A Look and unscramble.

1 dinwy

2 noswy

3 cdlouy

4 gygof

B Complete the puzzle.

C Look and write the answers.

hot   warm   cool   cold

sunny   cloudy   rainy   stormy   windy

1

How's the weather on Monday?

On Monday, it is *cool* and rainy.

2

How's the weather on Tuesday?

_____

3

How's the weather on Wednesday?

_____

4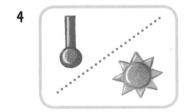

How's the weather on Thursday?

_____

5

How's the weather on Friday?

_____

This Week's Weather

Word Box
cloudy
sunny
Wednesday
On
report

Sarah reads the weather 1)_____.

2)_____ Monday, it is hot and sunny.

On Tuesday, it is warm and 3)_____.

On 4)_____, it is rainy and windy.

On Thursday, it is cool and stormy.

On Friday, it is hot and 5)_____ again.

E Read the story again and choose the correct words.

1 This story is | fiction | | nonfiction | .

2 This story is about | Sarah | | weather | .

3 It is | hot | | warm | and sunny on Monday.

4 It is cool and stormy on | Tuesday | | Thursday | .

How much do you like the story?

9

A Look and write.

look at flowers   read books   play in the snow   go to the beach

1 _____

2 _____

3 _____

4 _____

B Match and write.

ski

sled

spring

pumpkin pie

pick

winter

1 _____   2 _____

3 _____   4 _____

5 _____   6 _____

C Fill in the blanks by using the words in the boxes.

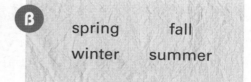

A make pumpkin pies   sled
look at flowers   play in the snow
go to the beach

B spring   fall
winter   summer

1 They _____ **A** _____ in _____ **B** _____ .

2 We _____ **A** _____ in _____ **B** _____ .

3 They _____ **A** _____ in _____ **B** _____ .

4 We _____ **A** _____ in _____ **B** _____ .

5 They _____ **A** _____ in _____ **B** _____ .

D Listen and fill in the blanks by using the word box. ⊙ Track 41

Seasonal Activities

Word Box

boys
in
make
enjoy
play

What do people do in each season?

The girls pick strawberries 1)_____ spring.

The boys 2)_____ in the rain in summer.

The girls 3)_____ pumpkin pies in fall.

The 4)_____ ski in winter.

They 5)_____ all of the seasons.

E Read the story again and choose the correct words.

1 This story is | fiction | | nonfiction | .

2 In spring, the girls pick | apples | | strawberries | .

3 In summer, the boys play in the | rain | | snow | .

4 In | fall | | winter | , the girls make pumpkin pies.

How much do you like the story? ★ ★ ★ ★ ★

12

Look and write.

| do homework | practice the piano | play hide and seek | bake cookies |

1  _____

2  _____

3  _____

4  _____

B **Trace and choose.**

1 soccer   ⓐ    ⓑ    ⓒ

2 meet   ⓐ    ⓑ    ⓒ

3 bake   ⓐ    ⓑ    ⓒ

4 tired   ⓐ    ⓑ    ⓒ

C Fill in the blanks by using the words in the boxes.

A
play   practices
meet   bakes
does   uses

B
soccer   the piano
cookies   my friends
his computer   her homework

A   **B**

1 She _____ _____ after school.

2 He _____ _____ after school.

3 We _____ _____ after school.

4 She _____ _____ after school.

5 He _____ _____ after school.

6 I _____ _____ after school.

D **Listen and fill in the blanks by using the word box.** ⊙ Track 42

Busy! Busy! Busy!

We are busy $^{1)}$ _____ school.

I play soccer after school.

Olivia meets $^{2)}$ _____ friends after school.

John practices the $^{3)}$ _____ after school.

He $^{4)}$ _____ does his homework.

Becky $^{5)}$ _____ cookies after school.

We are so tired.

E **Read the story again and choose the correct words.**

1 This story is | fiction | nonfiction | .

2 Olivia meets her | family | friends | after school.

3 John practices the | piano | violin | after school.

4 Everyone is so | tired | hungry | .

How much do you like the story?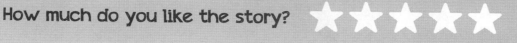

Chapter 3

Unit 06 Fun Activities

A Look and write.

blow bubbles   go bowling   ride bikes   play board games

1 ____________

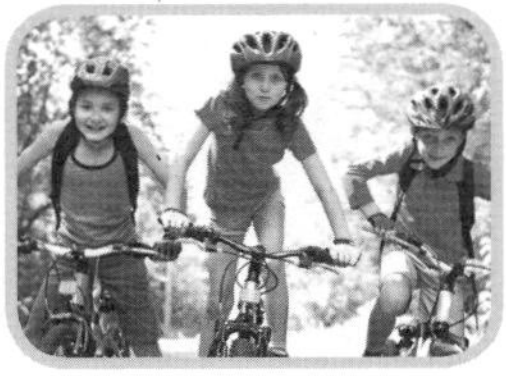

2 ____________

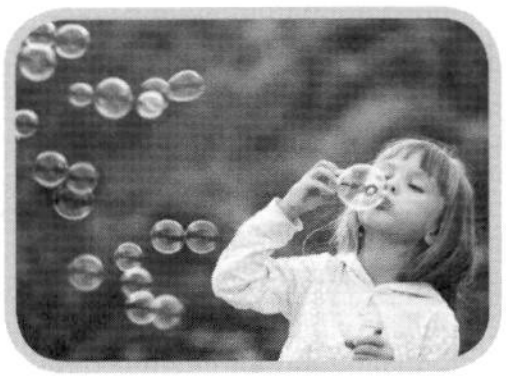

3 ____________

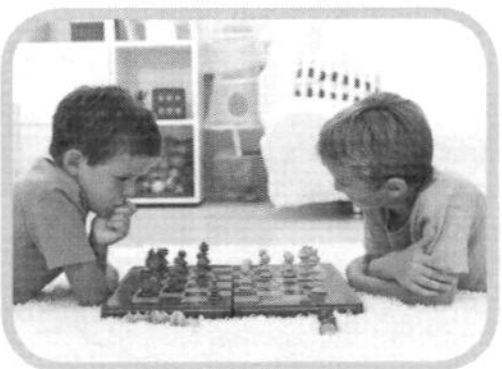

4 ____________

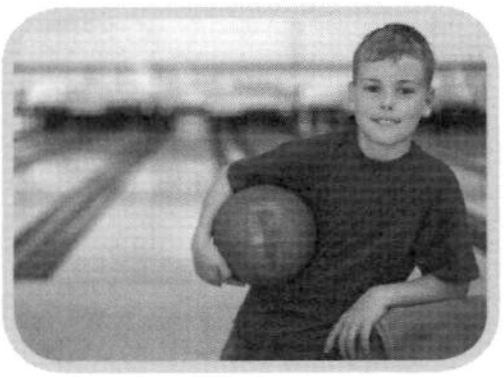

B Trace and choose.

1 cook
ⓐ
ⓑ
ⓒ

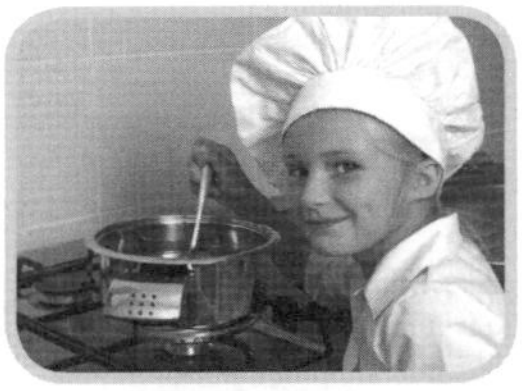

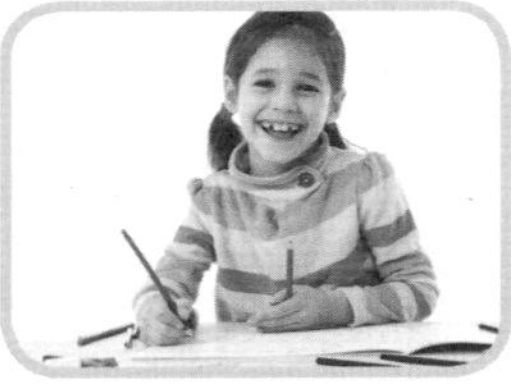

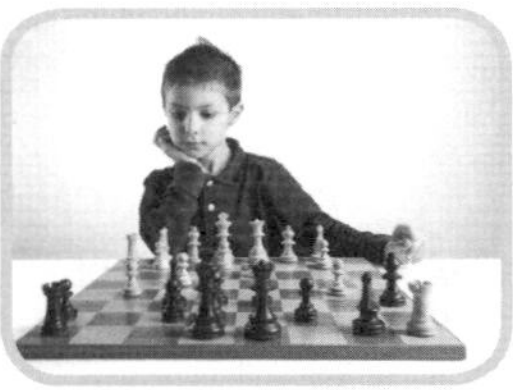

2 cartoon
ⓐ
ⓑ
ⓒ

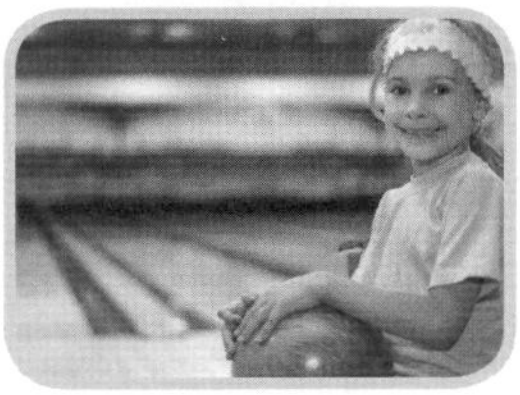

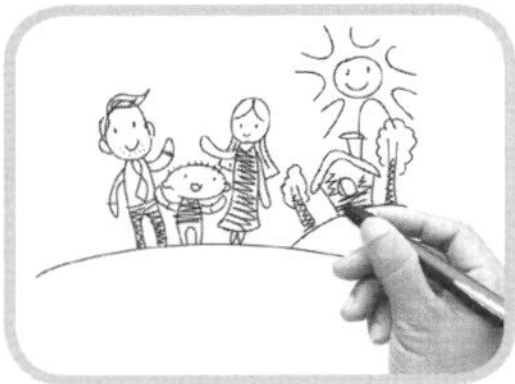

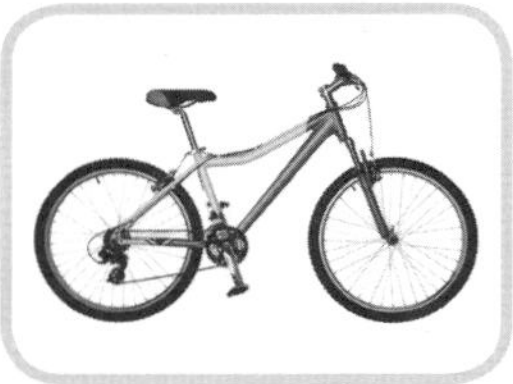

3 fun
ⓐ
ⓑ
ⓒ

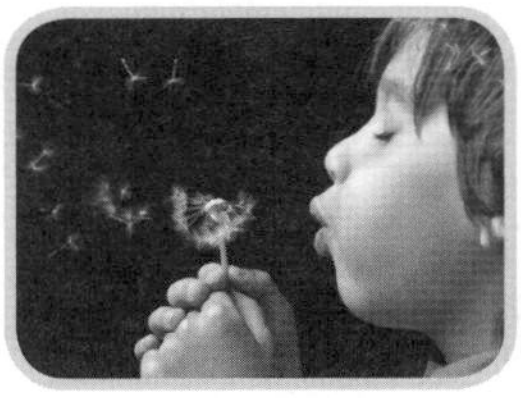

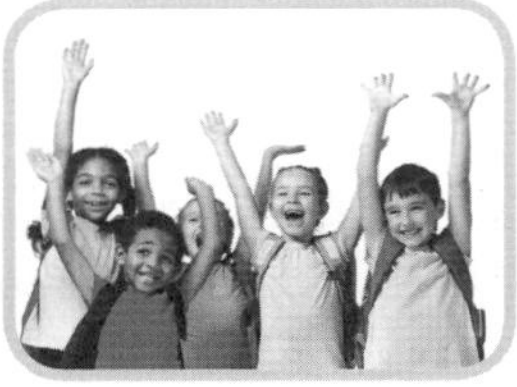

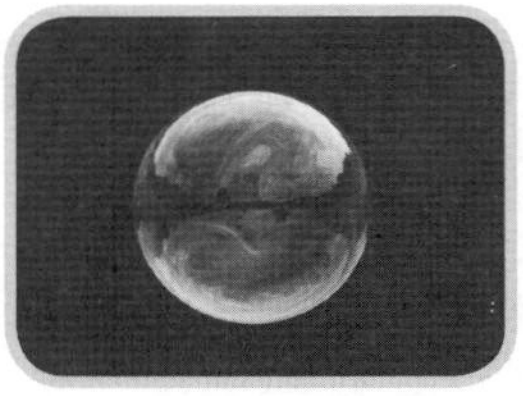

4 board game
ⓐ
ⓑ
ⓒ

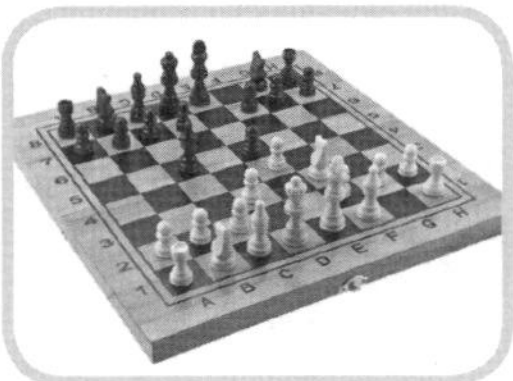

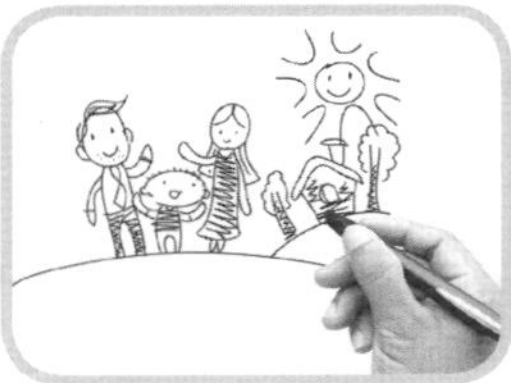

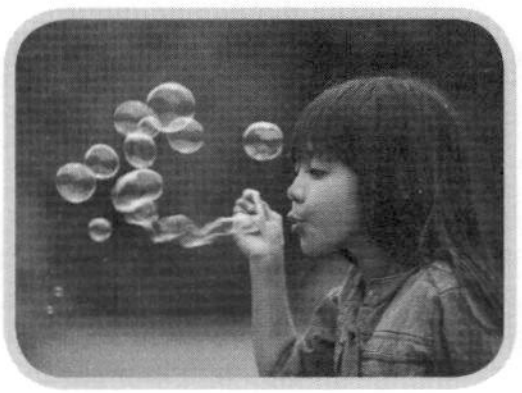

C Look and unscramble.

1

bubbles blowing She likes .

She likes blowing bubbles.

2

like playing They games board .

_____

3

cooking He likes .

_____

4

cartoons drawing like I .

_____

5

They bowling like going .

_____

6

bikes They their riding like .

_____

D Listen and fill in the blanks by using the word box. ⊙ Track 43

Fun Things

Word Box

much
also
like
cartoons
girls

There are many fun things everywhere.

The students all 1) _____ blowing bubbles.

They 2) _____ like drawing 3) _____.

The boys like riding their bikes in the park.

The 4) _____ like playing board games.

All of the activities are so 5) _____ fun.

E Read the story again and choose the correct words.

1 This story is fiction   nonfiction .

2 They all like blowing bubbles and drawing cartoons   going bowling .

3 The boys like riding their bikes in the park   house .

4 The girls like playing computer   board games.

How much do you like the story? ★ ★ ★ ★ ★

18

A Look and write.

| fish in the lake | have a picnic | go to a water park | go camping |

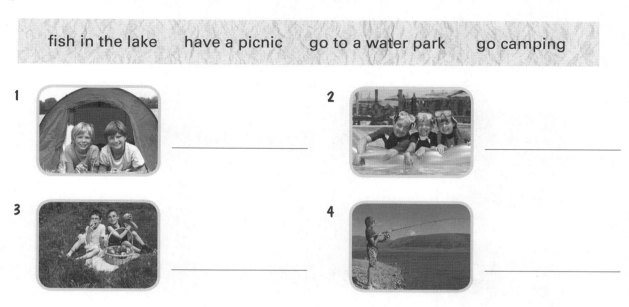

1 _____

2 _____

3 _____

4 _____

B Match and write.

1 _____

2 _____

3 _____

4 _____

5 _____

6 _____

C **Look and unscramble.**

1

the   throw   Let's   Frisbee   .

_____

2

a   Let's   picnic   have   .

_____

3

camping   go   Let's   .

_____

4

kite   a   fly   Let's   .

_____

5

the   Let's   in   fish   lake   .

_____

6

go   a   to   Let's   park   water   .

_____

D **Listen and fill in the blanks by using the word box.** ⊙ Track 44

A Day Out

Word Box

Let's
very
playing
not
throw

Tim and Mary are at the park.

They like ¹⁾ _____ outside.

"Let's have a picnic," says Mary.

"Sorry. I'm ²⁾ _____ hungry," answers Tim.

"Let's ³⁾ _____ the Frisbee," says Tim.

"No, it's ⁴⁾ _____ hot, let's swim," answers Mary.

"Great idea. ⁵⁾ _____ go!"

E **Read the story again and choose the correct words.**

1 This story is   fiction   nonfiction   .

2 Tim and Mary are at   school   the park   .

3 Tim is not   happy   hungry   .

4 Both Tim and Mary want to   swim   have a picnic   .

How much do you like the story?

21

A　Look and write.

Christmas　　Thanksgiving　　Mother's Day　　Father's Day

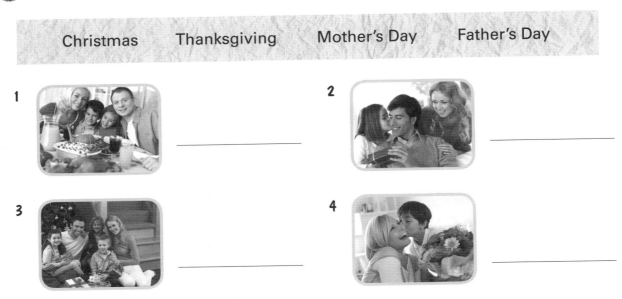

1 _____

2 _____

3 _____

4 _____

B　Match and write.

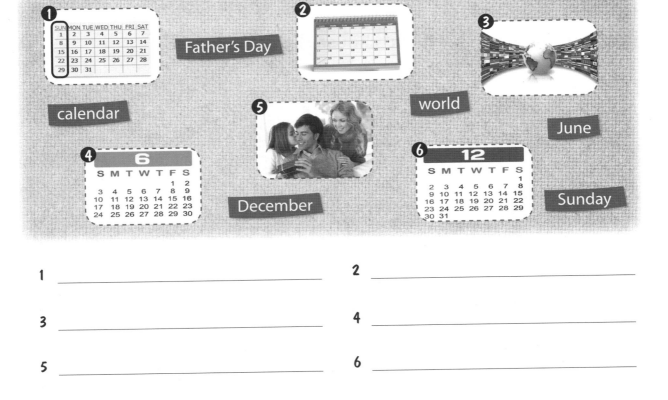

1 Father's Day

2

3 world

June

4

5 December

6 Sunday

calendar

1 _____

2 _____

3 _____

4 _____

5 _____

6 _____

C Fill in the blanks by using the words in the boxes.

A June   January
May   November
December

B Thursday   Tuesday
Wednesday   Sunday
Monday

1

S	M	T	W	T	F	S
	①	2	3	4	5	6
7	8	9	10	11	12	13
14	15	16	17	18	19	20
21	22	23	24	25	26	27
28	29	30	31			

A New Year's Day _is in January_ .

B It is on Monday.

2

A Christmas _____ .

B _____

3

A Father's Day _____ .

B _____

4

A Thanksgiving _____ .

B _____

5

A Mother's Day _____ .

B _____

23

D Listen and fill in the blanks by using the word box. ⊙ Track 45

Holidays

Word Box
Monday
Tuesday
January
look
June

There are many holidays around the world.

Let's ¹⁾ _____ at the calendar.

New Year's Day is in ²⁾ _____ .

It is on ³⁾ _____ .

Father's Day is in ⁴⁾ _____ .

It is on Sunday.

Christmas is in December.

It is on ⁵⁾ _____ .

E Read the story again and choose the correct words.

1 This story is | fiction | | nonfiction | .

2 January has | Father's Day | | New Year's Day | .

3 Father's Day is on | Sunday | | Monday | .

4 December has | New Year's Day | | Christmas | .

How much do you like the story?

24

A Look and unscramble.

1 elufhpl

2 tarsm

3 rvdier

4 accho

B Trace and choose.

1 librarian ⓐ ⓑ ⓒ

2 principal ⓐ ⓑ ⓒ

3 builder ⓐ ⓑ ⓒ

4 great ⓐ ⓑ ⓒ

C Look and unscramble.

1

is She friendly nice and .

_____

2

and Mr. Lee kind is funny .

_____

3

and is helpful smart She .

_____

4

Ms. Beaton and is funny nice .

_____

5

friendly is and He helpful .

_____

6

is Mr. Baker and smart nice .

_____

D **Listen and fill in the blanks by using the word box.** Track 46

School Workers

Word Box
great
kind
school
nice
Mr.

Furi loves the 1) _____ workers.

Mr. Zoozica is Furi's teacher.

He is 2) _____ and smart.

Ms. Poppet is the principal.

She is funny and 3) _____.

4) _____ Mookle is the librarian.

He is friendly and helpful.

They are all 5) _____.

E **Read the story again and choose the correct words.**

1 This story is | fiction | nonfiction |.

2 Furi's teacher is | Mr. Zoozica | Mr. Mookle |.

3 The principal is | kind | funny | and nice.

4 The librarian is friendly and | small | helpful |.

How much do you like the story?

27

A Look and write.

| field trip | sports day | graduation | bake sale |

1 _____

2 _____

3 _____

4 _____

B Trace and choose.

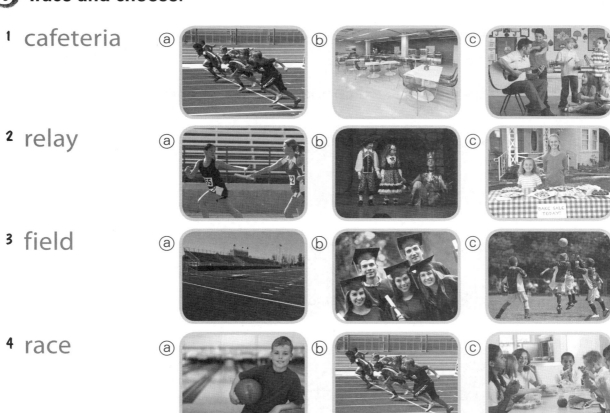

1 cafeteria ⓐ ⓑ ⓒ

2 relay ⓐ ⓑ ⓒ

3 field ⓐ ⓑ ⓒ

4 race ⓐ ⓑ ⓒ

C **Fill in the blanks by using the words in the boxes.**

A relay   bake sale
       basketball game
       race   talent show

B   on   in

1. The _____ is ___ the gym.

2. The _____ is ___ the playground.

3. The _____ is ___ the field.

4. The _____ is ___ the cafeteria.

5. The _____ is ___ the gym.

D Listen and fill in the blanks by using the word box. ⊙ Track 47

Sports Day

1) _____ is sports day.

Get ready. 2) _____. Go!

The races are on the field.

The 3) _____ game is in the gym.

The students 4) _____ lunch in the cafeteria.

The relay is on the playground.

5) _____ day is great for everybody.

E Read the story again and choose the correct words.

1 This story is | fiction | | nonfiction | .

2 This story is about | sports day | | relay | .

3 The races are on the | playground | | field | .

4 In the | cafeteria | | gym | , the students have lunch.

How much do you like the story?

30

A Look and write.

eat cotton candy	take pictures
drive bumper cars	ride on a roller coaster

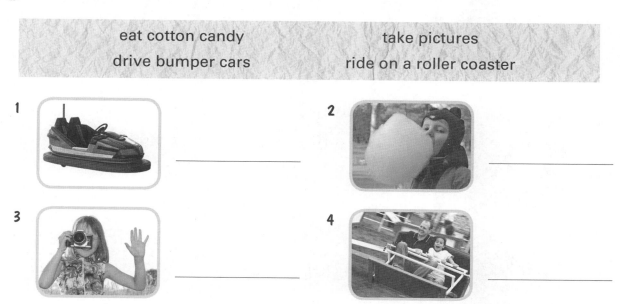

1 _____

2 _____

3 _____

4 _____

B Match and write.

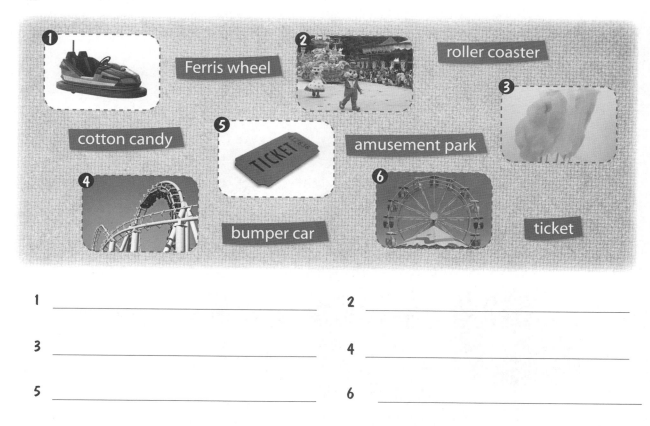

Ferris wheel

roller coaster

cotton candy

amusement park

bumper car

ticket

1 _____ 2 _____

3 _____ 4 _____

5 _____ 6 _____

C Look and unscramble.

1

am   I   taking   pictures   .

_____

2

cotton   She   is   eating   candy   .

_____

3

They   smiling   are   .

_____

4

buying   He   tickets   is   .

_____

5

is   Sam   car   the   driving   bumper   .

_____

6

are   riding   on   roller   the   coaster   We   .

_____

D **Listen and fill in the blanks by using the word box.** ⊙ Track 48

The Amusement Park

Look! We are at the amusement park.

I am not 1)_____ tickets.

I am 2)_____ a bumper car.

Mark is riding 3)_____ the roller coaster.

He is 4)_____.

Amy is eating cotton candy.

Oh! It is very 5)_____!

E **Read the story again and choose the correct words.**

1 This story is   fiction   nonfiction .

2 The children are at the   park   amusement park .

3 Mark is   smiling   crying .

4 Amy's cotton candy is   sour   sweet .

How much do you like the story?

A Look, choose, and write.

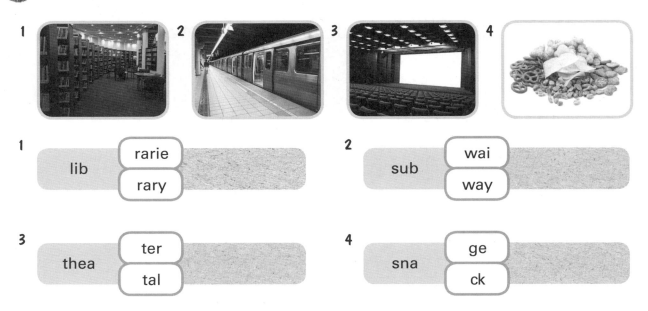

1

lib	rarie
	rary

2

sub	wai
	way

3

thea	ter
	tal

4

sna	ge
	ck

B Match and write.

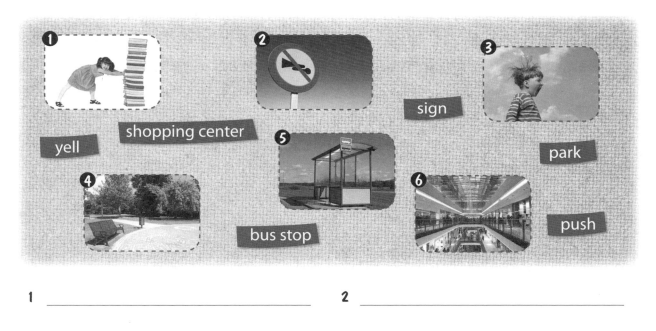

yell   shopping center   sign   park   bus stop   push

1 _____   2 _____

3 _____   4 _____

5 _____   6 _____

Look and write the sentences.

| yell | eat any snacks |
| run | fight | take pictures |

1

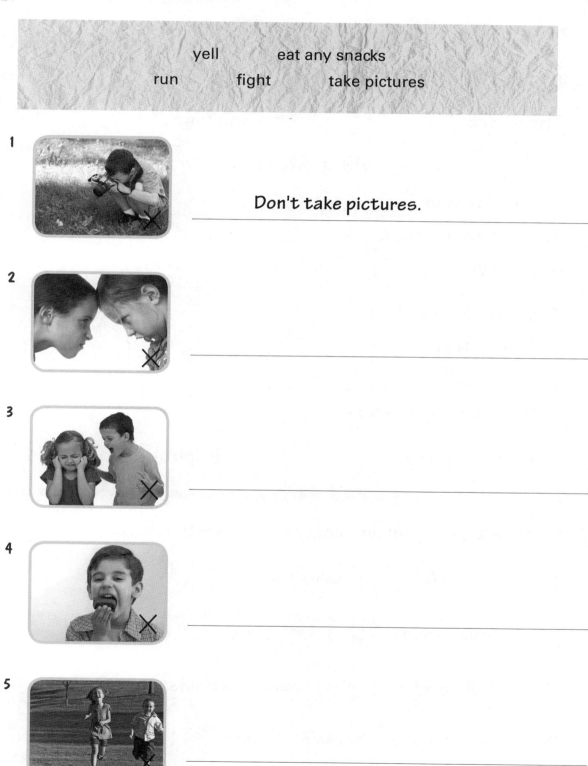

Don't take pictures.

2

3

4

5

D Listen and fill in the blanks by using the word box. ⊙ Track 49

Good Manners

There are 1)_____ on the sign.

<2)_____ a Bus Stop>

1. Wait for your 3)_____.

2. Don't push others.

3. Don't yell.

<At a Library>

1. Walk quietly.

2. Don't talk 4)_____.

3. Don't eat any snacks.

Let's have good 5)_____ in public places.

E Read the story again and choose the correct words.

1 This story is | fiction | | nonfiction | .

2 A bus stop is a | good | | public | place.

3 Don't | walk quietly | | eat any snacks | at a library.

4 Wait for your turn at a | bus stop | | park | .

How much do you like the story?

36

Winners' Reading & Writing is a seven-book course specially designed for learners of English from beginner to intermediate level. It has been developed to help learners dramatically improve both their reading and writing skills. Learners will experience stories covering a number of genres that are both interesting and informative. Following this, learners will be able to create a concrete piece of writing which will incorporate the target patterns. *Winners' Reading & Writing* will allow all English learners to develop the ability to read freely and to write with greater confidence.

Features

- Organized guides to every stage of reading and writing
- Providing a number of vocabulary categorized by various themes
- Introducing diverse genres with fun and educational stories
- Dealing with core grammar patterns for ESL/EFL learners
- Writing Point sections with sufficient exercises to develop accurate writing

Components

Student Book / Workbook

Downloadable Resources at http://www.clueandkey.com

WINNERS' Reading & Writing Series

- WINNERS' Reading & Writing STARTER
- WINNERS' Reading & Writing ❶
- WINNERS' Reading & Writing ❷
- WINNERS' Reading & Writing ❸
- WINNERS' Reading & Writing ❹
- WINNERS' Reading & Writing ❺
- WINNERS' Reading & Writing ❻